*Kinetic*

**Also by Michael Ayres:**

*Poems 1987–1992*
*1976 Streets*
*The Sky That was Your Guide*
*a.m.*

# Kinetic

Michael Ayres

Shearsman Books
Exeter

First published in the United Kingdom in 2007 by
Shearsman Books Ltd
58 Velwell Road
Exeter EX4 4LD

www.shearsman.com

ISBN-13   978-1-905700-43-1

ISBN-10   1-905700-43-1

Copyright © Michael Ayres, 2007.

The right of Michael Ayres to be identified as the author of this work has been asserted by him in accordance with the Copyrights, Designs and Patents Act of 1988. All rights reserved. No part of this publication may be reproduced, stored in a retrieval system, transmitted in any form or by any means, electronic, mechanical, photocopying, recording or otherwise, without the prior permission of the publisher.

**ACKNOWLEDGEMENT**

Many thanks to Tom Wilson for cover artwork and design.
Image copyright © Tom Wilson, 2007.

The publisher gratefully acknowledges financial assistance from
Arts Council England.

# Contents

| | |
|---|---|
| Stratosphere | 9 |
| Zero-G | 10 |
| Jet-lag | 12 |
| Nothing | 13 |
| Shimmer | 18 |
| Point | 20 |
| Helsinki | 21 |
| Sleep-state | 24 |
| Satan | 25 |
| Lightfast | 26 |
| Stars | 27 |
| Dragonflies | 28 |
| Heaven | 29 |
| Lightning | 30 |
| Downtime | 31 |
| Turbulence | 32 |
| Missing | 33 |
| Wait | 34 |
| Echo | 35 |
| Taishan | 36 |
| Hard | 37 |
| Impasse | 38 |
| Saigon | 39 |
| Zeitgeist | 40 |
| Indochine | 41 |
| Karma | 42 |
| Cuban | 44 |
| Ghostwriter | 46 |
| Czars | 48 |
| Desert | 49 |
| End | 51 |
| Sway | 53 |
| Cronos | 55 |
| Someone | 57 |
| Ladybird | 58 |

| | |
|---|---|
| Drive-in | 60 |
| Downstream | 63 |
| *rainman* | 67 |
| Flight | 71 |
| Stills | 75 |
| Summit | 76 |
| Provincial | 78 |
| Plateau | 80 |
| Stranded | 83 |
| Trashed | 85 |
| Crane | 88 |
| Jetstream | 91 |
| Kinesis | 95 |
| Vapourtrails | 98 |
| Seventeen | 102 |
| Want | 103 |
| Quake | 104 |
| Regime | 105 |
| Borne | 107 |
| Mobile | 109 |
| Tadpole | 110 |
| Cusp | 111 |

*Kinetic*

# Stratosphere

Like a plane in the stratosphere
seems to be moving slowly, but it isn't really

it's moving very fast you said
*Hey, it's a really good view from here*

# Zero-G

So the plane began to carry me away from you
*That's immaterial* someone had just said
and the word fluttered in my mind like a single petal
come loose from a blossom twists in the air
I felt as if I might never see you again
I couldn't hold you in my arms in the sky
We climbed and banked out over the ocean
then went into the clouds
Now I have to deal with the sky
One of your kisses
is the silence up here
after the vapour trail has faded

You were in an old moss green silk dress
I stroked your arm
You knelt on top of me
*Did you know that silk is stronger than steel* I said
*Then why don't they build skyscrapers out of it?* you asked
You kissed me
so we wove what we had from a moment
I wondered what the thread of that kiss could bear
Later, I found out

I was dreaming
The deer in the woods, one of them, a stag
with the face of an old friend
Even when I woke
I felt light-headed
and the day passed with the Zen seamlessness of dreams
There was a deer in the garden
nibbling at pine shoots
You phoned me
and suddenly I was filled with sky

At high altitude over China
I heard your voice
when you were in tears
We've passed through oceans together
and been rolled for years among the waves
I didn't understand
why there was no salt left on our skin
no taste of it
not a single grain

In thought's zero-G
above the clouds
the skyscrapers float empires drift deer graze
among the constellations
of stars and stars
which have no names
The cities left behind the cities to come
caught in the night flight
look the same
lit webs of memory
I missed you so much
I couldn't get back to you
There seemed no end
to a love that was homeless
to a love that had once been home

## Jet-lag

What is that bird?

Where does the bridge lead
which leads into nothing?

I hear you moving in another bed.

I want to melt like ice,
beginning at the edges,
ending at the clear centre
which is everywhere, softly.

What is this shadow?

How did the light get in?

Whose is that voice, calling?

And that sound…

Is that my voice? Is it rain?

# Nothing

You need to wake up
and I need to sleep.

Then we change round:
I need to wake up,
and you need to sleep.

I lay my head down on its side
to dream of you,
fly an airliner into the pillow,
depressurise over the desert,
slumped senseless at the controls,
passengers unconscious in their seats
glide on for hundreds of miles
and when I wake
you are lying beside me…

I need to love you
and I need to stop loving you,
I want to be near you

and far away,
arboreal regions
something cool in my blood
the hot dawn of Singapore
meltdown of the native

check my watch,
check the date, check my pulse,
bullet train in the evening,
empires and client states
a phantom of airports
words on a tannoy
we never heard

remember
some seashells
don't sound like the ocean at all

*Without love* you were saying

All the time
something is breaking,
something only whole
while it is breaking,
we have become
voices and echoes
disembodied or cropped
the video-con.
the link-up with Chicago
the damage which builds
sampans and buddhas

ties the dawn tight
to the sound of streetcleaners
vans with orange lights
hosing out the gutters,
the thing which is breaking
binds the streets to the evening
the cooks outside the back
of the neon-lit restaurant
open the bins
throw the garbage of my heart away

It's noon where I am
I think
almost midnight for you

you sound tired,
later I'll be tired

we're working shifts
they're different shifts

I begin to age quickly
in order to be real.
And when I'm real,
I'll thread myself on my fingers,
take off my bones, one by one,
they're heavy like memories,
leave them like pebbles
the children collected,
put them back on the shore,
pick up my passport,
take a high-speed train
anywhere you are,
everywhere you left,
I need to be with you,
I need to let you go.

*Without love*

How did something so hopeless
become filled with hope,
bomb craters and water,
craters on the moon,
how did something so desolate
become a vow,
a truth to be honoured
with all the lies we could tell?

You need to be sure, you say
you need to be certain
when you leave
all the lights are off

You need promises, security
you need to stay young
I need to kiss you
Some shells
are full of the sea

I need to write to you.
I'm turning into sand,
a desert of pale blue,
maybe it's more peaceful out there,
maybe there's no peace at all,
when I read your handwriting
I stroke the lines of the letters
trying to trace my way
back into your fingers

A storm here
but quiet where you are
the wind funnels and searches
a Goliath without Davids
Mermaid in the fish tank
a string of bubbles rising
past the pirate wreck,
I need to give up,
I need to be realistic,
I want to kiss you
and undo every day I have ever
been alive…

*Don't be stupid* you're saying
and *Without love* you're saying
above my head
satellites went gliding
with your voice in space

This room
is still years ago

There's dust on the sills
no bulbs in the sockets
*Don't be stupid*, you're saying
*Without love, we are nothing*

# Shimmer

I was in love with you, it made everything shimmer.
And it seemed as if my life grew real — by which I mean, insubstantial.

Skyscrapers like cobwebs; suspension bridges, gossamer...

When things give up their right to stay, the enduring pose,
and take off their cocoon shells, and flash and fade,

pulsing dust and fire, it's your love, executioner...

Everything grows provisional like footsteps. Rome and thistledown:
your fate is huge and fallacious and innocent, without you,

a child with a shell to their ear, hearing the ocean.

There were endless showers that summer. *Please stop, please stop, please stop* the wipers asked the rain as we idled at the crossing.

The lights were on red, but there was no one around...

Later, in America, we broke down in the desert,
and needed to change a wheel in the simmer of the heat-haze.

I rested for a moment. The mountains turned to your voice.

You were singing to Aretha on the radio: *I say a little prayer...*
Things had already begun to take off their masks:

chrome was melting into little iridescent green crabs with scarlet eyes...

Desiccation and erosion: memory is a badlands.
I hardly noticed, I kept trying to grow things

though Mao had gone and dust coats the hoardings.

There were scraggy palm trees outside the Dunes Motel.
I think of it even now, those asphyxiated palms, your perfume,

the way the jade teardrops in your lobes shimmered in the breeze.

Again, it ripples across the years, and my present stalls.
Somewhere, the rain is about to fall,

and your voice turns back into mountains.

## Point

Tonight, you are the nearest and most distant thing for me.
And in this place, only I know your name.

I have carried you for years and for miles, and they are the same.

I have come to the end of a thought, of a love.
When I forget your name, it will be lost forever.

At the point, I saw clouds moving through space, I don't know why.

# Helsinki

You wrap the night in your body.

You die slowly and after you die
spring comes. You twitch back to life again,
and spring comes.

In the sweetness lie the ashes.

You wrap the night in your body.
Its baby fingers curl in sleep, sungod,
tomorrow we will wake
I will lie beside you,
perhaps I will really have been born this time.

They slaughter the fairies using double-headed axes,
and nail the angels by the hair to the trees.
Spring comes, I am dying slowly.

In the blood lie the petals.

After I have died, I meet you again.
We don't say much but walk for a while in the heat
along the road which leads away from the airport.
The sky is a dull, impeccable blue,
so blue it cannot go on for long
but must die.

Yet, for a little while, it doesn't die,
and I am in love with you.

The Earth rotates upon its axis:
the full moon comes up and begins to glide across the sky
so on the ground the shadows of things begin moving.

You wrap the night in your body.
You unwrap the night, I lie beside you,
I look across the pillow into your face.
This morning is definitely the morning of my birth.

I've been lost for years,
wandering across a life like a plain,
watching ice form, watching ice melt away.

At a café with a friend, near the bus-station,
snow lay all around, white and pure,
but with the immaculate emptiness of a platitude
although still the flakes kept on falling.

Time drifted away.
They asphyxiated a witch, her black hair fanned on the pillow.
The freezer was full of the body parts
of dismembered princes.

But we are in love.
The night wraps us in moonlight,
we carry bundles of shadows
and in our kiss
each shadow gives birth to a flame.

In the silence lie the words.

I live slowly. We ripen and flee, hand in hand,
through a wood where all the shadows
fill slowly with snow.

You empty my body.
Out pours the night, snow,
the concrete buildings of Helsinki.

Out pour the car-rides through rational suburbs
planned not for oblivion but for memory.
Out pour the petals and the flames.

Summer comes, we are long dead.
I am numb with a wisdom which grows
progressively more useless,
increasingly hard to destroy.
I unwrap the day from my body,
put it on the table:
a salt cellar, a couple of knives and a key.

In the moments lie the years.

Cars drive through the slush.
The seas dry up
and the landscape is one of beached hulls and wrack,
and above the acres of stinking mud
the air is stirred by the moans of expiring mermaids.

# Sleep-state

Rain's precious attrition.
I am not with you.

I'm falling through cracks in between the moments.

Cool, icy bars of fluorescent light at the station:
the promise of an oblivion withheld

I drift in a sleep-state.
Sunflowers, smoke of Moroccan blue,

the articulated cream of trains crossing the fields at night,
a scarecrow with a gun.

At times, I regretted sleep, because sleep
deprived me of thoughts of you.

I don't want to waste a single thought of you.

Storm. Cloud over the plains.

Moment by moment, my love for you builds.
It accretes in red wellingtons and loose strands
of white-blonde hair, platonic and ordinary,

like single drops of rain
accumulate an element, a place we cannot escape

or deny, which in the end
we simply assume, which outlives us

as our lives: in my diary I wrote
*Tuesday: in Broken Edge, no rainfall for over two years*

*I dream of torrential storms.*
*This is a man.*

# **Satan**

*Satan, don't cry. It will be alright, you'll win again, one day.*
*Just not this day.*

I was on the train to London,
and I was thinking of you.

And so I became greater — quieter, you know,
more expansive, magnanimous.

Like rain, brushing my face.

Do raindrops possess shadows?
I guess they must do.
I suppose it must depend on the amount of light,
and the speed at which the raindrops are falling,

but I imagine life is like that —
the few instants when raindrops
move towards their own shadows.

And she said: *Is that the way thoughts move?*

Between the bombs and autumn.

Between a sigh and a murmur.

Words,

between our lips.

# Lightfast | 07.07.05

I wrote this poem for you,
and I wrote it in lightfast ink.

These are my speed trials.

These are hands, washed in black water.

Vapourtrail of a jet, bisecting the sky near dusk:
vapourtrail over your shoulder, and you said:
*Write me something about journeys.*

I said *Okay: I'll write a poem about a children's race,*
about the one who always gets left at the start.

I keep the photo of that skyscape.

The gathering dark.

The fading stars.

## Stars

We look up at the night sky
the same thing which flaws our hearts flaws the stars
the fluttering imperfection
which keeps things restless
The stars shine and beseech
they're so full of wanting
as we put them down
and kiss
their redundant light
flakes and scatters
I grow careless
with you in my arms
I already have the sky
We can count the stars later
We can forget the stars now

# Dragonflies

God was saying something to me
but I nodded off and when I woke
all I saw was the pale fume
from the spout of a kettle.

We walked by the ocean
white spray and blue waves like out of a Hokusai,
did you know that this species of dragonfly
has been on the Earth for three hundred thousand years
longer than us?

So they tore down the buildings I loved,
and they put up buildings I hated.
*It's okay* you said. *It's okay.*
*You just have to let go.*

It only takes the piano
five notes out from silence
to break your heart.
Sometimes I think that's because
you know the silence is always waiting,
sometimes I think
the music knows it, too.

I told you I loved you.
You told me how, once,
when you were young,
your mother cried and cried
when you went missing
lost in a field
chasing after dragonflies.

# Heaven

It seemed straightforward. The directions were easy.

But rooms grow quiet and the crowds disperse,
a kiss.

You were dead for a long time
until I found you.

Bedroom, or hotel room.

I kissed you, your skin was pale blue.

*Will we be happy?* you asked.
*Sure, why not?* I said.

Waiting room, or private room.

The crowds flowed as crowds do,
frothing at the edges,
but then no one remembered these words,
and the music grew louder,
covering the sound of the fire.

I kissed you, and there were children in that kiss:
children, airliners, tomorrows…

Railway station, or departure lounge.

The walk up the slope, through the trees…

The sliding doors and the escalators…

But rooms grow quiet, and the crowds disperse.

When we got there,
heaven was empty.

# Lightning

Lightning, and you wait for the thunder.
Somehow she seems fused by the appletree in blossom,

but there are the years.

You think: so much space caught up in one little love.
The millipede of the lightning writhes, the petal falls,

and you wait.

# Downtime

You're not going anywhere for a moment.
The screen has frozen blank like a fuselage.
The hands of the little clock go round and round
but they're measuring nothing.
Later, you'll go somewhere.
In a while, when things start up again.

Tiger Leaping Gorge is to be dammed and flooded
and the realm of the lost is inside me,
just an edge of it, nowhere near my heart.
The stars grind, the wind over the city grinds,
the leaves of the morning glory in the little pot
are being ground to powder.
When the storm breaks, car alarms and burglar alarms
go off all down the street.
All the crucial things of life have been neglected,
but at least all the trivial things are in place.

I want this moment to end, and it does.

# Turbulence

You slept and the clouds slept inside you.
I watched you while you lay there,

and the storm broke and didn't wake you.

I thought, *How can all that turbulence be still?*

The body is a vase full of empty space.
Storms happen there, but even the storms are small

compared to the emptiness, which yet isn't peaceful.

You poured me out, now I have no corner of the world
to rest in. I was awake while the storm blew,

though you slept through it, with clouds inside you.

You left me while I was dreaming of the moon.
I was walking on the lunar surface, in a shower of rain.

You're still leaving me. I'm awake. It is still raining on the moon.

# Missing

Condensation on a window
is a field of atomised silver
and three droplets run down
random *kana* near the centre:
they are darker
like fluent steel,
they look like signs,
but they are not signs.

*No God, but the meaning of God*
the treatise says.
*Why do you bother writing?* you ask, gloomily,
staring out at the spring rain
which cages us with fertility.
*I'm not writing, I'm waiting*, I say.
I'm not writing, I'm in love.


In the generation of Lord Katsushige there were retainers who, regardless of high or low rank, were requested to work before the master from the time they were young. When Shiba Kizaemon was doing such service, once the master was clipping his nails and said, "Throw these away." Kizaemon held them in his hand but did not stand up, and the master said, "What's the matter?" Kizaemon said, "There's one missing." The master said, "Here it is," and handed over the one that he had hidden
— *Hagakure*, by Yamamoto Tsunetomo, trans. William Scott Wilson

# Wait

I will wait.

And when you've gone
the day will close both its eyes
but won't sleep.

Rain will fall, slowly.

Pearls will form — so slowly.

A wave will rise no one will ever see.

A wave will crash in silence.

Rain will fall, slowly.

And then I'll rest
my head on my right hand
and close both my eyes
like two pearls forming.

And when you've gone,
the day, tired out with chasing waves,
will try to be night,
and even if it sleeps, won't sleep.

I will wait.

# Echo

I was so tired, but I waited for the words
which would bring me to you.

And the wait was a gape of air, but no breath,
lightning near a dry horizon,
you said, *I'll be there soon.*

It was the very last day of May,
a phone ringing in an empty room by the sea.

I thought *Waves are the way*
*the sea connects itself to the shore.*

I was so tired, in that empty room,
no phone ringing.

And the river empties itself into the sea
perpetually, without effort, and I waited.

I love you, like the river, like the words
which don't come, like the storm
which doesn't break.

In July, there was hardly any rain.
When I picked up the phone, it was hot from being in the sun.
*I'll be here*, I said.

# Taishan

Slowly, my wishes became monuments.
When she pressed her lips against the tissue
a slit of lipstick was left,
a Rorschach butterfly
in Rouge Mysore —
such a fragile detail,
and when we exchanged a kiss
it was desire for order,
the tissue falling into the bin
like a wounded snowflake.

*Don't*, she murmured.

The party was boring,
another room in the house of regret,
an opulent mansion, filled with strangers.
I wanted to go back
and lift the tissue from where it had fallen,
a keepsake of almost nothing,
the stuff of life.
Instead, we talked about politics and films,
ice-sheets and global warming.
We made our excuses and left early
but the forecast blizzard never arrived.

In the car we listened to music.
*Held you tight but, darling, couldn't hold you*
the singer crooned. A commentator
said the characters engraved on the Taishan monument
looked like white sunshine
after the showers of late autumn have passed.
We don't know the real beauty of the Taishan characters
because the stone monument has fallen apart
and not even a rubbed copy is left.
And still, when we drew up outside our house,
there was no snow.

# **Hard**

I said that words were the hardest things in the universe
but you weren't listening. I lapsed into silence

watched traffic go by. You struck a match.

I thought about yesterday, then I thought about today.
You said something about making a decision.

The smoke from your cigarette dispersed slowly, starting from your lips.

# Impasse

We reached an impasse and fell back into ourselves
I remembered I didn't know the names of the flowers
in that small spot of silence
You hooked a curl of your hair away from your ear
I began to feel lost and the motors driving the universe
began to slow
and all my life felt worth
was the movement of nameless flowers

You turned half profile and the light melted around you
Another and a colder light
glinted on icebergs and there was no one to see them
If you could touch me now
none of this would be necessary
But the hands which move through memory
have no feeling and sometimes
even they slip under the surface and fade

The tall pampas grass in the railway station swayed
so gently it looked as if it were filmed in slow motion
Still we didn't say anything
or make a movement towards each other
Instead we made loss blossom
In the silence between us
things grew imperceptibly like crystal
Your fingers lifted to tether back your hair again
All the time
I brought in the flowers to show you
but I didn't know their names

*We should go* you murmur
but we make no move
For a moment in the stillness
I see icebergs glittering across the ocean

# Saigon

Adrift in an ocean of memory: old man, look at your hands.
But you have no hands, you are not here,

you are remembering, a lotus which opens, beginning at the core.

Water sprinklers surprised you, weaving lush snakes in the humid garden.
A scent of rotting bark, a growth fed on decay:

she said, laughing: *Try to forget me. Oh, no — wait: I'm unforgettable!*

The petals open in a way like crowns,
but the edges burn quickly and their whiteness tans:

and you reach for a newspaper with a warning of war.

# **Zeitgeist**

We made love. I felt at once tender and affectless.
We sighed and were no one, for a little while at least.

They were helicoptering people up off the embassy roof.
*Reizan reizan reizan...* The whir of the rotors,
the whump and cackle of the blades as they went airborne,
the passing quietness of the sky once they had gone...

I know, I said I would love you forever.
I wasn't lying. I meant it at the time. I just didn't realise

forever doesn't last that long.

## Indochine

You disposed of me quickly, efficiently, one neat phonecall.
That's cool. I guess you had your reasons.

Did you know, Yesenin wrote his last poem in his own blood?

That's not my style. I'm more Zen, more detached.

I'll never write a last poem.

# Karma

*Poetry won't save you*, Lord Ryosomon said.
*No, but it will make me beautiful before I die*
the coolest swordsman replied,
flicking open his fan.

I put down the novel when you phoned
Somehow I never picked it up again
and your voice was lighter than the first rain of spring
It was the rain and the breeze carried away the cherry blossoms
*We could meet up* you said
I guess it was your voice carried me away

Do you lie in the stones you've thrown
skimmed over the ocean
in the faces you've touched with the tips of your fingers
does something remain?
Is there one thing or are there many things going on?
When eyelids you've kissed open
my eyes look up across the city
the skyscrapers are brushed by your scent and the sky
takes longer to dissolve in the dusk with you

The album was achingly hip
though the singer's voice was empty
Some say that worlds go by like trains
when journeys forget their makers
Sometimes when you switched off the light
and we lay in silence
the darkness seemed broken

Slowly the parts usurp the whole
and we grow small, divided
If we are so divinely ineffectual
to be ourselves and no more

it's okay
but nothing will matter
and the stones resting on the seabed
the ones we threw there
will lose all memory of us
of a touch that was never ours
of a warmth we never had

# Cuban

I hear your voice
in the voices of other women
complaining about the rain;
and I hear your voice
as clouds pass over the waterfall
when the waters turn blue,
then black, then blue…

When I am near you
there is a place inside me
the breeze can go,
there's a hotel in my spine,
someone strums a guitar,
the guests are wakeful
and I can't sleep.

When you brush past me,
it's night and people are talking
in quiet, low, warm voices
fumed with coffee and wine,
reminiscing of their own country,
far off at this moment,
in the hemisphere of daylight,
and I can hear them
in my back, in my wrists
and under my eyes,
I turn over,
I can't sleep.

When you look at me,
it's all I want,
and when we're apart
I try to reach you in memory,
stars buried under my pulse,
geese through a V-lite,

a breeze filled with footsteps
brings me gorgeous anxiety,
you make me restless,
marooned in the early hours,
I hear the voices of exiles
murmuring from balconies,
remembering their homes
on breath hot with rum,
snow falls on Cuba
as I try to reach you
in an empty hotel
where no one is dreaming
and even the ghosts
can't sleep…

I turn over and the light on my skin
and on my eyes
is the light of a dawn
which never seems to fade
until it fades.
And when I touch you
then fingers stop still
on the strings of a guitar
and the guests fall quiet
as if they are listening.

I hear your voice
in the voices of bored women
complaining of the weather
and in the lulls
when the women grow silent
in the hush before morning
I hear my love
being carried towards you
like memories of home
on the backs of the rain.

# Ghostwriter

Like the bang and dazzle of Ginza,
thrashing light and signs
the train tilts and a strand of your hair
slides against my cheekbone,
this is the place I wanted to come,
I don't know my way out of here

We walk across the moon of a moment
it grows stars in clumps
the stars set or die, I don't know,
they are no longer there,
the face in the mirror rises like a sun
no one knows who is inside it
but dawn happens anyway
the light flows in like a tide,
darkness bared strangers
and the light covers them
both the strangers we met
and the strangers we were

Milk settles into calcium,
Columbus lies in his cradle and cries,
Satan sleeps and his pager is silent
no one needs him
corals form on the floor of our room
the wind carries the scent of smoke
from the chrysales of our burning houses
butterflies rise and take the breeze

One by one, the moments close their doors
I'm summoning the courage to kiss you
Acorn as a bullet
on the palm of my hand
and a forest in gunshots

On another train, gliding through Germany
to the wheep, chuckle and hush of a subtle electro
it's not a place I wanted to be
Somewhere along the line
the years have grown mountains

Cities of glass tremble and slide, flicker and dither
How many people live there?
I turn to kiss you
but it's just a glitch, a stutter of pixels,
a whisper of memory
I can't find my way out
I can't find my way in
can't find my way back. In Ginza
my book says
*Men should be the colour of cherry blossoms,*
*even in death*
but this isn't Ginza
I am not the colour of cherry blossoms
This isn't spring
I am not dead

## Czars

I wore a dark suit with a white shirt no tie
and I was unshaven
Nick took some head-shots half-lengths profiles
I pore over □△O Zen signs of the universe
the greens on the film were especially vibrant
electrified ferns beside the falls
with a sheen of New Zealand musselshells
as if everything had been lying underwater for years
or had become coated with glowing lichens

That winter had a Siberian feel
the frosts and drifts thick and luxuriant like boyar beards
You lay on the sofa lit only by a coal fire
At times the earth froze so hard
they found it difficult to dig graves

One by one, our moments became gaols
The secret of them was locked inside
No one visited them
And I do not go back to my own life,
except sometimes, in these words

Slowly our last kisses formed landscapes
the cruelty and the love in them places we come to
fetch up upon like coastlines
and when I dream I walk through a petrified forest
I kiss you again and think I can leave you

Some empires just fall others need to be dismantled

*If you think there's a secret in the snowclouds,
there is you said.*

*But then, maybe they're just snowclouds.*

# Desert

We threw snowballs. The day was crystalline, you know,
every facet of it was clean and sharp
so that it somehow drifted to stillness.
Your absence is glacial:
there's something monumental about it.
We ran and abandoned our shadows
or thought we did.
Then our shadows came back in, fast, like waves.
Some of us were caught and froze
as if we were children.
All around us, ferns were growing.
At zero degrees, ice and water
come to a new arrangement.

We asked for a moment in which to rest our love
but there was never a moment.
So we loved without rest:
there was a place we had to arrive,
but first we always had to travel.
Gradually, the place we built was a journey.
No one can stay there,
it's always the moment
the airliner noses above the clouds
into widescreen moonlight.
We arrive in suspense,
adrift in phosphorous.
The way home is now lost. For us,
there is only the way into the maze
of our kiss.
We never come out again.
We go in, but only strangers leave…

A magical uncertainty grips us,
we keep our children inside nutmegs,

rolled in leaves of mint,
and stable our horses in chargecards and glances.
We only know the bud's interior
when the flower blossoms.
All over the world tonight
people open to emptiness.
Inside everyone
lovers stumble out like tired dancers.
The air is sunken with the scent of honeysuckle
and the dancers
walk home to their disparate suburbs
to execute themselves in mirrors: tomorrow
they will be dark and secret again —
*Trust me*, she says

*Nothing ever seems to happen in this town* we yawn
and the politicians make no progress
on the important issues of the day.
Our love builds like storms, it builds
then somehow the storm has passed
without any violence at all.
So we get to be beautiful again,
as the temperature hits zero.
What approaches us now
moves only very slowly
like a massive, golden desert dune.

# End

Sometimes I wonder if we'll make it to the end
you left without a word so we were strangers again
with just little strands and echoes of friends left inside us
Perhaps one day when you wake, I'll wake inside you
even though, here, I've been sleeping for years and still sleep
As if you wake to snow falling
while I sleep late into the sun

A volcano in your mouth extinct for years
and our eyes like smoke which have drifted in glances
far from the point of original fire
Of course we're just the latest in a long line of lovers
who break up and don't quite understand why
The path through the woods seems to come to an end for no reason
and we wondered why people made it at all in the first place
Perhaps they didn't know that one day they would wake
alone to see the sky grey and snow falling
rare in that climate and soft like the first note of a quiet
piece of music
Perhaps they just liked walking and had nowhere really to go

You wake drunk and depressed
You are hibernating in summer but you remember
the golden darkness of your youth
It's cold where I am and the faulty streetlight flickers off and on
like a scene out of *Eraserhead*
There is something clinical about these streets
and it's not just the snow
In the drifts, smoking traffic begins to take on a mammoth inertia
I kissed you so hard I cut my lip on your teeth
blood like lava
The light comes on full and the street is lit like a theatre
I carry you sleeping inside me
I keep walking, quietly, so I don't disturb you
If I woke you, I would cry

You sleep late into the cool darkness of the sun
You love this piece of music just exactly where it ends
You open your eyes and for a moment don't know where you are
There's a sudden thaw and a river I once knew
blossoms into echoes
I untie my bundle of memories and lie down again for the night
You murmur a song right into my ear
it's softer than a flake of snow upon your eyelashes
I love this piece of music

# Sway

Do you think that to understand fire you have to burn?
Something titanic and unsettled fills the air this time of year
sways slowly in the turmoil of the willow trees
the wind blows the branches
they will never be still again
They never have been still
I feel uneasy in their presence
My life is in them
It's just May and the wind blowing the willow trees
so they hiss and shimmer
Is it this easy to get lost forever?
Is this what I have wanted forever?

I have forgotten the steps taken to get here
It's a bridge one by one the planks melt behind me
As I walk the bridge extends across the emptiness
More and more melts away
When I look back I see the willow trees ahead of me
When memory fails the emptiness returns
The emptiness, the fullness
Like trees returning to a clearing
Or ice refreezing a path made by breakers

There are things I never said to you
The important things
I said so many trivial things
Somehow the moment never came
Now I watch willow trees swaying and rolling in the wind
In May with this silence in my mouth
silence in the jugular and under all the veins
Now the moment has finally come
but we are not there to meet it
Instead I must go down alone
into the vast silence of the heart
and ask and ask again

The way even to the questions is fading
magically under the trees
It would be the same with the answers
The bridge to them melts to emptiness
It's the same with everything
The bridge melts to emptiness
and the emptiness melts into your eyes
So here you are again
And wasn't there something I wanted to say to you?

He came from a hard background
His horizons were limited
and love wasn't easy for him
But when he heard the music that day
something happened inside him
While the cello music played there was something he understood
He felt his horizons tremble,
all of them, all at once,
and he felt as if all the dimensions of his world
could expand, perhaps there would be a fire…
As the music played, he felt he could understand
There is something inside the music you understand, always
but when the music stops playing
you stop understanding

And he didn't understand
that the music
always stops playing

# Cronos

Take me into you
When the wheels and the spindles turn so that time comes on
*That old watch is like a beetle* you said
*with ticking legs and a golden shell*
*It's a gift* I answer
And Adrian said: *"Gift" is the German for "poison"*
Fix it into me
Slip it in... And, slowly...
Take me out of me...

We put our lives through the mill of a kiss
a few hours of it anyway
I moan and sigh I can feel things being ground down
the bones I woke with this morning
crushed and a little blood come out
Our kiss mills diamonds
and the dust of them filters out
useless and glittering and cold
At least I know what I want now
At least I know what there is to lose

You lay me down
I was in a car-smash so I belong to you
It uses its licking scalpel on me
cutting away
Saw through
into the cavity of the chest
to feel all that plunder
and take it out, jewel by soft jewel
*Does it hurt?* you ask
but there's still too much of me
*Does it hurt too much?*
*Don't stop* I murmur

So take me into you
We'll take the great and grind it down
slowly relentlessly we have the will and we have the need
and we have the time
We'll leave an ash tip leave the smouldering embers
an epic landfill where the tractors rut on garbage
and the gulls wheel
leave the craters on the moon
Get traction on me
Put in your straws put in your tongue and turn and sigh
Begin to syphon off my life
that's what I want from you
Didn't you teach me after all
there is an infinite number of things upon this earth
an infinite number of useless things
which are not you
and don't lead to you
So why would I want to waste my life on them?
You waste my life instead
We'll leave the reckoning to someone else

Like this azure sky
Like thoughts about love
Like thinking you can make it alone

## Someone

I lay on my back in the grass looking up into the heavens.
Someone shook the world like a snowdome beneath me

violently, so it was winter in New York.
When you bent over to kiss me,
for a moment you seemed to bite the sky.

# Ladybird

*Maybe tomorrow* you said
We slipped away into dreams we didn't remember
and woke into lives we guessed were our own
The coroner walked through the snow
and the mortuary was buzzing
We had come to our new hotel
and everywhere there was gossip,
voices rising and falling
like the movements of a sea
People sit up and lie down
They come erect and keel over
When we sleep we all sleep in the same darkness
but we think we wake to a different light

I couldn't get my body to work
couldn't reach out for you in the old way
and the words I wanted to say never formed
only white jasmine or ladybirds
or the squeak of guitar strings late at night
in bedsits where the students play to their shadows
and their future somehow recedes for a while
before they sleep in their special darkness
reserved for the young, the unique and the gifted

*We could put it off for a while* I said
He was in an accident and suffered a trauma
Why aren't we afraid every morning we wake
into so giant a void with its unknowns and the light
seeping through our eyes not the light of yesterday but new?
*Where am I?* he asked
*It's okay. It's okay* they said. *You're safe. You're home...*

Sometimes the divine amnesia lifts
and I remember how it was when you cried

My limbs have drifted away from me
*If I've done one significant thing in this world*
I murmured, stroking back the hair from your face
*it's that I've loved you*
and you smiled when the train went past
a ladybird landed near my eyelid
*Ladybird! Ladybird! Fly away* you whispered

# Drive-in

Vincent was looking good
in a cool steel grey suit
and a white shirt
gliding through Los Angeles at night
meaning to kill some people.

I couldn't get into the film.
You know how sometimes that happens.
*Sure, it's like your own life*
you said to me once:
*It's like the inside of any one moment.*

Nocturnal L.A. shot from above,
the place light comes to die,
elephant,
a liner going down under the sheer weight
of its own radiance,
and in the silence between us
carbon dark palms
shimmer to silhouettes at dusk
while bellowing mammoths raise their tusks
out of the tar
but make no sound.

Reflections gleam in the dinosaur chrome
as the limo prowls by.
*What about Maui?* you ask.
Along the freeways
cars assemble their endless line
in a glamorous cortege
the drivers solemn with vacuity
and all the time the city weeps in gasoline —
but doesn't, in fact, weep.

We were not involved.
The dead glided by with the eerie fatuity
of figures waving from carnival floats.
I had no time for the victims
or for the star,
I wasn't interested in motivation or fate,
and felt no overwhelming need
to map all the details
of the complex infrastructure of his soul.
It all reeled slowly past,
the lawns, the sprinklers and the pools,
your laughter, your smile.

Guides to Hawai on the table.
Jet skis, and waves, Wakiki, snorkels.
I don't know if we were trying to escape
certain complications in our relationship.
When we kissed
I had an uneasy feeling
if we would slide our fingers
along the edge of our lips
our skin would be stained with rust.

It was a drive-in movie.
Blood began to flow
like a visual oil
but we didn't make the end of the show.
A flash of guns, the wasteful barrels,
I had a feeling of *déja-vu*,
the gore spilt on the limestone tiles
of the expensive hotel
was like a crimson seed.
Your attitude was indolent *bushido*.
*People have always died* you said,
*and they always will.*

*We could try Polynesia*, you suggested.
*Wouldn't that be cool?*
*We could fly out tonight.*
We didn't go, of course,
not to Tahiti, not straightaway,
but we kept talking about it:
in the background, the film kept playing
and the lights kept burning
on angels, bored with heaven.

# Downstream

We could lie to each other now or tell the truth
turn to each other or turn away
Downstream of our love perhaps there is a new life stirring
Upstream we are young and the light of the day
less used

Crowds gather all the time there are more of them
and they are growing in size
Slowly people begin to wheel and flow
drawn into the crowds by a kind of savage inertia
Fireworks over the bridge gunpowder galaxies and snow
We could lie with each other now
or tell the truth
We could turn to each other
or turn away

We pause for a moment on the ridge
and watch titanic summer clouds move over the hills
their shadows glide with a divine seamlessness
The clouds do not touch their own shadows
but are responsible for them all the same
I feel you close there is just a little sky between us
for a moment forever
We pass into the shadow of cumulus
and live our lives beneath its ephemeral fortress
Downstream of our love perhaps a new life is stirring
Upstream we are born and our eyes open for the last time
unused

Shut the doors shut the blinds the night is so vast
Turn into ourselves pause for a moment and wonder
then settle and sleep when the world turns over
and something is lost
Crowds mill and thrash
and begin their descent into herds

Whether we kiss or not is becoming irrelevant
we will run with the herd and where the herd stops
we will stop
Upstream I am walking away from you
though I could still turn back
I could still care for others
Downstream I could live for you
but I can't

Meanwhile we murmur in the darkness in the morning wake
perhaps pause for a moment and wonder
perform the chores we call ourselves
ride the trains and wipe the mirrors
maintain the routines where the hours go by
and yet all the time in secret
we tend to a desolate grandeur
the toppled pillars the grate of the wind
the weeds which twine
Upstream the spring has come and the days are swelling
Downstream we're not speaking because we're so tired and all the lies
have already been told

Upstream our lips touch for the first time
and in the red light of that kiss
ghosts are born and swarm like moths
under the flowering cherry trees
Upstream the world unfurls like a bud
There is a greenness such a green
there are many leaves and small succulent sounds
of flowing water
Rain drips on a stone
We have the world to ourselves and we belong in this place
Belong to it still
and believe we make it beautiful

Upstream we get in late put on the heating and a record
Town was busy with Christmas shopping
*That is so you* I say
*It IS so me* you say
We crack open a bottle trawl through the freezer for meat
You have a new dress I have a jacket
I show you the Japanese print I just bought
You kiss me hard but I don't feel like making love
For a moment though
I feel the phantoms of cherry blossoms in my mouth
and hair and scent them on your skin
We don't bother with the news
and turn off the tv soon after
Sleep comes in waves
and the days pass

We emerge from the shadow of the cloud and are grateful
Its fortress has fallen another one is rising
Upstream of our love perhaps a new life is stirring
Downstream of our love an old life ends
a new coldness begins

Downstream the roots are exposed and the soil eroded
the trees are withered

Downstream the cattle kneel and drop their bones
the abandoned gather
no one calls

Downstream the pledges and the promises fail
like the power
the will to live together
fails

In a heavy dream I walk under cherry trees
in spring

Downstream

# rainman | for Tom

There is something about a thunderstorm
Something... convincing...
Crossing heaven on our way to somewhere else
the storm came
and we had to break our journey
We sheltered under the same tree for a while, you and I
At the ruined gate of Rashomon
where the rain falls grey and silver
When the deluge ended
the people packed up the pieces of their stories
and melted away

Between the days of the swallows and willows
and the days of swallows and the waves
she came into my life
Her arrival and your leaving
somehow grew mixed up in my mind
This pink the Japanese call "the colour of change"
How wise they are
to see inside an evening train
where her lips are on mine
and the sunset of our kiss
brings out small insects drifting
and singing

So check out the samurai in the kimono
of horizon blue, *kame-nozoki*
a bottled sky
He looks so cool
striding through the whispers and drums
of a fragile electronica
He looks happy
He's so full of the spring
you'd think he might just
break into flower

My heart is empty
There are just a few thoughts lying around in it

like clothes in a deserted room
or petals on a lake
I'll miss you but there are always the flames of leaving
in everything
Stars come out in the water
they're only just born and are too stunned to cry
Maybe we'll cry for them, one day
if we find ourselves under a bookshop doorway or a tall tree
sheltering from a sudden storm

There's nothing to keep us here
The ashes of butterflies in the gutters
are vividly white when they take wing
and though our flesh respires and we make of ourselves
hands to reach and hold
all these things in the end are just made of wishes
I am not a geni and this world is not coming back
to life
You're not a geni either
We none of us are
but grant me this wish, anyway
Let the sunlight strike the buildings, just so
and the sky above us
be as it is
infinitely precise
on a day we smiled
on a day we didn't part

This section of the city is gentrifying fast
By the old mosque and the gay porn cinema
outside a pub with black and green walls
on a summer evening in a solstice light
and heat
there's a shimmer of temple bells
a Shinto of workbooks and spreadsheets
and Gen grinning in the rubble of Hiroshima
a young man resilient like the wheat

who carried his mother upon his back
to a place of vanishing
In a clearing in our dreams
we'll take the chance of beauty while we can
And all this stuff, this kit and glint and beer and roar
skyscrapers and railway stations, taxis and cranes
has the weight of dragonflies
reflected in slow-moving streams

You see it has the ominous grace
of a mid-air collision
In all this sumptuous void
like two planes approaching
a point of nothing where the cirrus hangs and fades
Sometimes I see my friends and lovers
lit up from within by the miracle of burning
I ask for the fire
and it is given to me
When I ask again
it is taken away

The departure lounge is quiet
In Yum-Yum's on the Caledonian Road
the fish float in their tank
but no one looks at them
Their gorgeousness has been laid off
Dust strikes
The summer is left vacant
the doors are locked
everyone's away
So she unties the sunrise from her hair
where the coral lives 400 years
and grows in clusters on the silent sea-bed
The colour of this dawn
is too delicate
even for flames to hold

My friend I remember the time we first met
On a train gliding into London
travelling light as you always are
The area's different now, not much remains
of the old quarter
the spraypaint on the walls has gone
Back then there were different tags you know
I used to see them every day —
things like *WHITE TRASH* and *rainman*

# Flight

No one remains where the rain takes hold
No one inside as we sleep but the murmurs of children
The butterfly has flown the cocoon is empty
Stroke the child Dracula's hair out of his eyes his fringe needs trimming
Tell him to rest sing to him hold him
Hold him
Hold him tight

There are no sounds anymore there is just noise
You cradle an empty cocoon on the palm of your left hand
and stroke it for a moment and stare
Then you look upwards
The sky is beautiful it will take all your gaze
Gaze all you want to
You look down and let the cocoon slip off your hand
The sky is still there
Turn away walk away
Set the controls for the heart of loneliness
Walk and murmur a lullaby

We have reached the end of love it was surprisingly easy
to lose ourselves and all we had cared for
No one remains inside us where the rain starts falling
The mobile is still and the nursery is empty
Touch the planes and make them fly
round and round and lift up and bob down a little
Take a flight ourselves to an accessible paradise
Set the controls
Depressurise over the desert and fly
Israelites and Egyptians beneath us
Murmur a lullaby as the squares empty
Luxor and Thebes Bosnia-Herzegovina
The end of love is surprisingly easy

There is no one inside us now the hard times are here
An anglepoise lamp and a book by Jacques Derrida
A sky which was open begins to close
A book which was closed begins to open
No need to envy Ahab his great gliding hearse
I guess we were on autopilot for years
There are no sounds anymore just a band playing ragtime
then they play *Autumn*
Strangers are coming to hurt us and demean us
Sometimes we are the strangers
We all need water and we all need shelter
Step outside look up at the starlight
Set the heart for the onset of loneliness
Let them come

Nature they say abhors a vacuum
No one remains where the rain takes hold gunshots
have emptied the square my temples are tingling
Our kisses grew hollow and lost their meaning
Love has its limits and I'm afraid that we found them
It's not hatred it's just that we must live
Strangers are coming to take what we have
but there is no one inside us to prevent or delay them
We are going into a slavery we devised
to fill the vacuum of a love which failed
A sublime hearse rears up out of the waves and glides
Here come the hard times
Walk towards them and murmur a lullaby

When little things fail the great things fall
Just ask the Dodo
There's no one inside me to fend off the techno and the tail lights
weeping blood in the rain like cheap digital
Strangers are coming to take what we have

but when they arrive in me
they'll find rain in a square nightfall spilt petrol's
random peacock graffiti
They'll find strangers like you and strangers like me
When the great things fall little things remain
the moon caught in a waterbead
Thirst
Longing
If they arrive in you
when they arrive in me

You brush the soil from your hands clap them
as if you're applauding
You rarely have soil on your hands these days
and the earth has drifted far off from you
The sky is still there
It has plenty of places for you
Start walking
The breeze will toy
with the fragments of a broken cocoon
There are plenty of places to go only
none of them will be home
That's okay
Perhaps in the end
we all turn back into strangers anyway
the same as when we were born

You keep moving
The sky will conceal you in its emptiness
and you will leave no trace there
like the people before you
The sky is still there
but the rain takes hold
and the wind picks up speed

You're cold now
when once you were warm
You stop murmuring the lullaby
Maybe elsewhere at this moment
a stranger hesitates
sees a butterfly alight then rise
wings opening and closing
in a silent applause
while we sleep among thunder
and wake in its storm

## Stills

Nick used tungsten film the colours glowed in the darkened room
Such light as there was was full and lush
as if it was going out of style
and the greens seemed to bleed and wash over themselves
while Nick snapped away we talked
listened to The Czars and sometimes we were quiet
I thought of you
a fir forest at the bottom of the ocean, trees
frozen with the birdsong still in them.

Later the clouds brought snow,
and I thought of the cold air blown in a wind from Siberia.

Yes, they were graves, so what?

And I thought it was a long way into my heart
but when you came to leave
I found it was just a short walk, after all.

# Summit

*One star, two stars, three stars*
You lean over me, way back
The dazzling years pass the darkness is still darkness
there are fewer years
the darkness is the same

We scoop up the ocean
carry it into our world of salt and leaves and cream
You run a little of it down your body
just for the feel
and because you can
When you cry
you agitate the surface
Like this, we can hold the ocean prisoner
and torment it
We kiss and torment

Are you counting the stars?
*Yes*

Yes, back to the stars
You shake your head
and the sinuous copper of your hair
flows with shadows
We will conquer the moment conquer the hour
and the years dazzle as they pass
We let the ocean go free
but it will just wander lonely and uncertain
A beautiful fatigue enters us
Deserts form and your eyelids close
Everything gets weighed in the terrible balances
everything learns how to be forgotten
and when we have conquered the years
your eyes open and I have gone

You cry
and the anguish seems so powerful for a moment
it appears not to belong to us
We slept so late
we missed the tree in its blossoming
and later still,
the petals lay around us
like a fertile rust

Each petal went into the balances
Each heartbeat against time
One star, two stars, three stars

## Provincial

*I don't know what I think, but I know how I feel.*
Yeah? So how do you feel?
What?... Now?
Sure. Right here. Right now.

So she turns away and he pulls her face back to his
and he kisses her.
Then they stare ahead
and the cigarette smoke comes out of both their mouths
in wisps, and looks like the smoke from the barrel of a pistol
or from a machine.

The landscape yawns.
I want you and I can have you
Raindrops fall in their millions
but each drop is individual
When the water drips into the drain
the life of the droplet is over

Cars join traffic
in the hot summer dusk
I know all the lights and I know all the signs
The mopeds flit like insects
but mopeds don't reproduce
My dream
has outgrown this place
so I cannot stay here
My dream
is greater than I am
Who would have thought
we could be crushed by the weight
of our own dreams?

After the gig
we hit the Pillbox.

You know the crowd. Damon was there,
Tracy, the others. We were shown straight in
past the hicks and the doorman and the velvet rope.
It's getting too well known,
it's no longer hip.
We'll have to move on soon
make somewhere ours and cool again
find somewhere less predictable.

Then he looks out over the citycentre
The fifth largest economy in the world
Rainclouds forming over the lights
The design of storms never changes

# Plateau

*You only get one shot at beauty* she said
Like the map of the Underground flattens out space
it was early spring
This world and all that was in it died long ago
Our reflections on the dimpled steel of the café table
facing in different directions
all the work of love
the cool flow of the river
the mist drifting fused with the water
the specks of black fleas on the cat
the silence between us

Soon we will be moving through an emotional landscape
of gulches and ravines
a place of pauses, dead ends, full stops
Our mouths will hardly touch
sometimes they will hardly move at all
Something sour and harsh will collect inside us
leak out of us and slowly flood the rooms in which we stand
Weeds will gather where the waters run and spool
beads will drip in necklaces like light-filled pearls
plaster will slump off the walls the walls
will crumble moss and ferns will begin to grow
where the bed is made and the pillows
are undelved by the shapes of heads
*It's not the end of the world, it's just the end of us*
you say and I believe you
as the floor dissolves beneath my feet
*Look, just wait. You'll see.*
*After certain death, living gets easier*

We break open the spring evening with a kiss
Inside me I'm trembling
and life turns gorgeously uncertain
My eyes are closed and I don't know when to open them

Your mouth feels so good on mine
it's a way into bliss
We don't know the way
There are no signposts this is not
an old path
I want to open my eyes and yet
that would mean we had reached the plateau
the climb was over and the heavens as close
as they would ever be
We're in hyperspace in April
Should I open my eyes, now?

We have made all the mistakes and all the houses have tumbled
The slates lie like the backs of books among the rubble
When a heron moves the water ripples and the moon
is quivered in its dream of sky
We have suffered the pain and caused the hurt
shepherded our grief to the place of loss
and so very, very carefully
assembled our loss one kiss one word one
tear at a time
tended it and protected it
called it the names of our children and our lovers' names
whispered in the throat
It has all gone

I can talk about the stars if you like
but things have evened out here
the days of spike and pulse are over
we know the truth and can live on into it
We don't want each other anymore but we need each other
We need what we don't want
Perhaps if we could recognise this state of affairs
we might learn to want each other again
Maybe we'll just hate our way across this endless plateau

where the stars really are
almost intrusive in their brilliance
The weight of their light crackles against sense
and my nerves stand up like iron filings
brushed by a magnet
You turn towards me and I can feel
our kiss beginning to form its cave inside us
We step across the threshold
you cut me loose from my name
and the dimensions of things begin to change rapidly
We stop kissing and you look at me with those cool,
affectless eyes
*You only get one shot at beauty*, you say

# Stranded

*There's too much beauty*
*It can break you this life*
*Sometimes you just have to shut down*
You looked worn out
shining and threadbare
like a glove
which has touched so many things
You looked plundered
You looked... beautiful...

Turn over the hourglass, it's the same sand slips through
How dull it must be
for the sand in the hourglass
waiting for someone
to need time

*I just feel I have no skins, you know*
*I become too porous*
*If you don't shut things out*
*they'll come to you for comfort*
*like fish to a lamp*
*just things cocoa tins nails and stuff*
*never mind the poor people*

We had a while before the flight
so we looked at our giant atlas
pointed out names
Black Sea Mediterranean Caspian
Middlesbrough Sydney
names which meant something to us
and names which meant nothing at all

The towers came up and the towers came down
Grand Old Duke of York Blues
I lay on the sand and gazed up

at a drifting Gondwanaland of clouds
I only knew you for a short while
I guess that was the only way with you
You weren't built for long haul
Staying around is almost my forté
outlasting oceans
or the ethereal wisps of your tears

*You just have to take care with beauty*
*with the world when it's like this I mean*
*When it's like you*
*beauty is dangerous*
*You mustn't swim out too far*
*but you have to believe in love*
*otherwise you get stranded*
*the tide goes out one day*
*beyond the horizon*
*and the waves never come back*

My bones feel loose inside me
the hands which caressed your face breasts
the powerful thrust of your shoulders and thighs
The memories were fresh like rushes
in the editing suite
almost like life itself
It was Bon in Hiroshima
and all around Japan
the dead had ridden in
on horses of eggplants cucumbers and reeds
At night they return to their land
in paper boats with lighted candles
set sail
on bodies of water

# Trashed

So we played our music to the ocean
I guess we were telling it we were beautiful
that this is what we could do
showing we were more than guilty
as the full moon came up and the batteries ran out
and the waves came on
and there was no more music
there was just me and you
Sometimes it's easy to get home
Sometimes, home seems far away

You were always the space between two glances
in a little piece of darkness I found there
Later we moved away from the sea
I failed into you and I remembered
hippie kids with their guitars on the beach
they'd made a fire from old peach crates
and it wasn't that I couldn't get back there
I just didn't want to

Maybe later they'd shoot up maybe they already had
You'd find needles in the sand
They were playing their music to the ocean
showing the night what they could do
You kissed my stomach
we lay on the rug
The palms rustled
and the waves came on

We hurt each other it's what we do
I kissed your hair how I loved your hair
when it was wet and slung across my chest
The water made your hair darker
when I lay on my back and we still had time
not to mess things up

I saw the flash but heard no thunder
It was all free but we stole it anyway
It was delicate and it came to us for protection
so we smashed it in hard, thoughtlessly
in our own, highly imitable way, trashed it
repeatedly relentlessly over the years
until we became a trail of cold debris
and even then it asked for mercy
so we hit it again
until at last it grew silent
It was so fragile
You were so fragile

We could love again and things would be better
We wouldn't have to cry like this
when we think of what has become of us
the dirt inside us and the pain
how we have aged and what we have lost
what we really wanted
what we still want
to be beautiful
We could love again and we could be beautiful
and I would still keep you there
if only we could rest for a little while
if only we could stop hurting each other

The girl who danced to the badly tuned guitars
in a tatty sarong
among the needles and the used condoms
the boy who played to her
they rested once in the arms of their mothers
long foal limbs
she lay her head against their heads and hummed
some dreamy tune

I'm restless tonight
so you pour back into my memory
a scent of peaches and smoke and sand
You made the crucial things happen
You took my last ride away from me
so we plundered the moonlight the dark clouds
cars moving along the coast road
then the moonlight again and then each other
Some beauty you don't have to pay for
but we pay anyway
We love each other it's what we'll do
Sometimes, you just can't get home at night
Some nights, you don't want to

# Crane

Like a tracking or a crane shot with that kind of glide
there is a surreptitious magic to it
One day half your life has gone
My wishes grew slowly up around me like ethereal trees
Now I'm moving through a spectral forest
of oaks and beeches which shine like thistledowns
I jam back the night with all I have left
I wish you were with me
and that wish is already overgrown
with the spindly shadows of the long summer evening
We have come apart and the pieces glow
Some tiny filaments of life remain
and we cater to those as we can
with something of duty, something of just plain hanging on
the way we observe the faces in photographs
as we clean the dust from them

We pass each other on the stairs
and glance at each other again as we did when we were just
a little younger
You're held for a moment in an embrace which seems
more powerful and more vital than time
Its fierceness hurts us
like looking into the sun
but even if we held on too long
and entered a darkness which contained years
the sunlight beyond our blindness would still be serene
would come when the sun rose
and fade when the sun set

You smile and say something cool and commonplace
and I smile back and say something simple and banal
but in those words and in that glance
great weather systems revolve over the world
storms build over China

and there is Russian snow inside you
and rusting railway tracks which vanish to nothing
bearing no trains for decades
but larksong which can burn down summer
When the glance closes and the words fall back into silence
I find I have come to the place again
within us all, a breathtaking nexus
of flight numbers and caresses
I say nothing and we pass
In the echoing stairwell
I hear the vanishing song of a lark

We wake again and are committed to flesh
It staggers us with its demands
one of which is forever to leave
If I didn't care for you it seems
I wouldn't care for much these days
but caring for you
I find I have a phone number which still means something
even to me

You make me feel
that what is lost now will be lost for all time
You make me wake into a life
which is irretrievably beautiful and even in the middle
of this searing indolence I want you
You bring loss close
so I can feel it
You make loss slow right down
to the beat of your sleeping heart
so I may watch over it
measure it out
Where we drift in a room which sways with light
and shadows, like a freight, like a cargo,
just before the photographs become real and their silver

coalesces into shards of past
we stroke against each other, just with our lips,
and find ourselves in glinting instants once more
bedazzled and hungry, bemused, wandering
into the place we will turn
to strangers and go,
we find ourselves again I mean
within touching distance

## Jetstream

I guess we've come a long way
from different sides of the world
to feel like we made it
to feel like we're free
Lie back on the bed
in the Dunes Motel
a full moon out the window
in the daylight
and the sky over the sands
white desert blue
The first moment I saw you
I didn't cross the room
I waited a moment
I knew it was important
then I crossed my whole life
to reach you

Samsonite luggage
stuff strewn round the room
sarongs from Bali
plane tickets from Rome
Memories from elsewhere
Spring in London
and on Judd Street
crushed black cherries from the trees
We're working together
to make something better
Blue collar honour
White collar love

*Listen, man, we're here to stay*
he murmurs and it's beautiful
He's talking of people
who haven't been broken
who haven't been bought

The drugs have kicked in
It's hot like a dying star
From the bar by the shore
the runway built in the sea
I watch the planes landing
in the twilight
and I watch the planes
taking off

If I didn't love you
someone else would
Maybe someone better
Probably someone better
But I've got the gig now
I crossed my death without thinking
just to reach you
Ask me
I'll do it again

You know, someone once told me
the brightest object in the universe
is the Pistol Star
I know when I kiss you
one day I'll think back
our kiss will be memory
But then, what isn't memory?
When I was with you
a few hours later
I thought of the Pistol Star
and when you made a face at me
I laughed

Houses on Fleet Street
Hotels on Mayfair
Petrol in the gutter

and petals from cherry trees
We're not here for the sorrow
not today, not for a while
Let others take the weight
we'll be sorry one day
We'll take our turn then
We'll take up the strain
Every summer is Troy
We have to burn it while we can
Burn it completely
There are plenty of Troys

We've come a long way
but we've a long way to go
The next moment with you
seems so distant
I wake with palm trees inside me
a breeze from the sea
It looks like a crime scene
passports and visas
cocaine by the bed
It's a heist movie
after the hit
We stole our moment
It wasn't ours to begin with
it belonged to the others
but we have it now
and we're going to keep it
Go back to sleep
with a snowstorm inside you
Indifference is cheap
and we can afford it

Emptiness of places
emptiness of lies

We'll fly out tomorrow
We have no ties here
no ties at all
the people are strangers
locals lost in their struggle
each scrabbling, scraping and little,
they're all the same
We'll wake somewhere else
We'll make everywhere elsewhere
We'll get there tomorrow
They say it's the bomb
a happening place
They say it's poor
backward, provincial
I don't much care
Blue collar greed
White collar shame
We've a long way to go
Leave it all in our jetstream

# Kinesis

So you come to a new place
Bodies in motion even sleeping you swing and sway
cities are built inside you
honeycombed with loneliness and the rumble of crowds
like tides coming in
Like tides going out
I dream of you lying naked on the bed
in an Indian summer
your body at rest except
it is in my eyes and in my dream
and there is moonlight in my blood and the charge of waves
where you sigh among white sheets and the storm rises
and the storm fades
When I wake I am in the past
The moon crumbles and the city falls
and there is just a scent of honey in the stillness of autumn
and no scent at all of the sea

Perhaps if you could lay out the atoms like beads
things would make sense
If you could take off the electrons and slip free
of all this strange commotion
in a silence where the vapourtrails form
Perhaps somebody could rest and really see
what's going on
If the song wasn't so lovely and the memory
so casually flawed
If there was a place you could keep the stillness
If there was somewhere you could really keep time

So you've come to a new place
You've carried a whole sky inside you gliding
A vase of tulips in America
a shawl in Islamabad at dusk
and in between a journey

Only, you can't sleep and you can't stop the journey
It goes on without you within you
We are only kissing
We are only saying goodbye
If there was a reason for any of this
If there was a real itinerary
a place you could go back to and check on things
If we had a motive for the stars
if we had an excuse or a credible alibi
perhaps we'd really be here
left high and dry when the foaming waves of our dreams at last
retreated and some kind of stillness was truly possible
Maybe I wouldn't need to lie to you
in my gorgeous, absent-minded way
Maybe I could really leave you
Maybe our dreams would mean something
But maybe not

You always wanted a fire which never burned
You always wanted to keep your geni in the bottle
but then somehow the magic happens anyway
and you find yourself in a strange city by the sea
walking in the harbour
wondering what happened
to a world you called home
The moon took it
The moon, and the flames you carry inside you
And the jets with their fading white traces of flightpaths
across a quiet sky
Meanwhile you're only half listening
as I explain why I didn't come/didn't write/didn't call
The skyscrapers glisten and shine
in their slow self-immolation
and the endorphins run low
and your friends, one by one, let you down

I'm telling you
you shouldn't have believed them when they said
that only those who have loved
can ever really be alone

For a while things seems okay then for a while
they're not so good but they're not actually bad
Then somehow the interlude grows longer than the play
I kissed you as if I was trying
to find my way back along invisible lines
to the moment we still cared for each other
There seems a soft map inside you
but we tear that up when we really make love
We turn away
Petals fall via Hong Kong
Dusk holds you, but not for long
Someone else holds you
You wake and the sky takes you
"Utopia", remember, means "nowhere"

# Vapourtrails

I could see the end coming
in the games of children
*You have permishion to use our garden*
and Black Mick and Mickula
the young girl
with storms forming over her white dress
stroking back her hair
as the stunned boy gazes on
in the supercharged air
right there at the origin
of the era of ferns

You have arrived late
in this exquisite summer
the great haunted skies
the long retreat
a Napoleon without Moscow
a few nights without sleep
It's Airbus days against the heavens
the slow fast lines of the vapourtrails
Your kiss your first silence
your lessons in tears
it's the speed of the city
into the crowd
the ache and the dream in desperate rooms
in every direction
fifteen steps from the Drug Tsar

It's not September
it's the autumn of autumn
Yours is the last beauty
You bring it dark to the evening
in a black dragon dress
Soldiers and graves

seem far off from these stars
You're so fresh to this world
you should be nurtured
shielded from disaster
of fire, weardown and whispers
but it's the wrong hour for miracles
time out for the superheroes
and not one warrior
among the amassed ranks of terracotta
will look into your eyes
or lift a single finger
to save you

Caesars come gawp at you
aloof in their dreamsleep
wake to the ruins
they think they can build
I drove in from the desert
full of oblivion
low on endorphins
and short of fuel
You don't need the past
and the generals
don't know what to do with you
At a scorched bus station
in Khartoum, Arizona
I'll write you a poem
which remembers the shore

You were made for the ocean
for the rain
and for running from the rain
You were made for the summer drive
There's such injustice
you've arrived out of time

you missed all the journeys
we made for you
Hijacked planes stand on runways
filmed for hours in their stillness
wings foreshortened in heat-haze
There's little hope
We fight on
in a war with no enemy
ruthless but blind
we crave our own sorrow
and now we have taken
the greatest hostage of all
and won't let go

Your love
is scattered summer to the roads
It should have been
a fifty-storey heartache
built and razed in four weeks
No need for Greeks or Egyptians
or towns out of seventies
AOR songs
Instead it's a struggle
the fag-end
of a once-gorgeous battle
It feels right that we meet
in these lost days
of the death of elsewhere
on the beach
by the ruined pier
under derelict stars
a few moments' peace
a foxhole in the heart
Outside
the way to tomorrow

narrows and grinds
and a damaged sun
shines in our eyes
The cabin door opens
A shadow appears
Our children
will live in fear

## Seventeen

One night we connected the moonlight with the starlight
and we held them together for a moment
Then they began to slide apart
We couldn't hold them for too long
and they couldn't hold us
We were only seventeen years old
Then we began to fall apart
It hurt me to think
someone else waited in the daylight
Now I understand
they were someone else to love
Now I understand
we had someone else to love

# Want

You know it's a mistake but you kiss anyway
What have you to lose?
Then the wave of the horns hits you
and you roll over and it's spring:
*Want to, want to can't forget you blues*

What gets kept and what gets lost I don't know
It all gets mixed up
litters the trail
Migrating swallows arc through you
taking their pieces of summer with them
and they sleep on the wing
In the end, no one gets to stay in the kiss
its soft tent folds and burns the moment you wake
up into each other again
The room seems emptier but then
it was the same before only safer
Other people will come and be happy here
and after all
most stars don't have names

# Quake

During the quake, the trees shed their blossoms suddenly,
a blizzard of jettison,
*flump!*

We were listening to music,
and it was as if I grew lighter.
The buildings juddered and fell in epilepsy,
the diamond clung to the vinyl —
and so it happened.

Streets on which the cherry trees stood
vanished, but that was just time.

Bombers droned overhead, streets vanished.

Love came suddenly, like rain.

There was devastation. Some people were really struggling.
They lost almost everything.
Then they lost everything.

Suddenly, like a shower of rain.

The stylus still glided in the groove.
Then there was no music,
because it had happened.

You lost me, slowly.

So, we picked ourselves up, and went on our way.

Slowly, as if we could still find a home
among the sighs and murmurs.

And as the city subsided in dust
the cherry trees blossomed.

# Regime

We didn't expect snow but snow came
We went outside into the difference it made of us
and walked for a while towards who knows where
In spring the shadows of briar leaves swayed on the wooden floor
You were always waiting for something
But what were you waiting for?
Sunlight by the sea tanned me I grew drowsy
One day I switched off my mobile somehow
I never switched it on again
We lost each other in a new love
a new lie or a new love
I walked outside into the distance it made of us
I never noticed we were losing touch

You wanted to make a place like an object
In the end I just used you you can admire
the beauty of a mantis as well as of a snowflake
You were always trying to rebuild castles that were fallen
In Japan we saw the place
where the river runs between two mountains
Between us between our bodies clouds drifted past
cars drifted past time and life drifted past
Regimes fell and others arose
Out of the bodies of lovers the world is always being made
and children dream of justice
We'll be used again and again because we make love
and children need power
You wanted a place like an object
I wanted a place to lie down

You lay seige to the moment you always want surrender
but it hurts to be forever at war
They'll break you at last for wanting to take and to hold
and they'll call the pieces status or duty
must-have essential must-see to-die-for
You'll do what they want because you want to
I'll leave you in the summer when it looks like rain

We didn't expect snow but snow came
It lay seige to us
For a while there was only snow falling where we had been
we didn't stop the wind blowing or combing up the waves
or the bodies of our children forming
It was spring and there were still a few months before I would leave you
We gave ourselves but they took us
They said they had to pay for us that was how it worked
but we gave ourselves anyway
I deleted your new number then I switched off my phone
but I couldn't delete your voice in my ear
We cried because children were starving
We cried but we didn't do anything
We were free but they bought us anyway
It was the nature of the new regime

Between our bodies clouds drifted past
briars grew by the open window
You prepare yourself to be left and to be used
Why will they never see?
You prepare your children to be used and to be hurt
It's hard to bear
such injustice
Now I'm alone laying seige to your memory
as we kissed cars drifted past and evening flights and trains
taking people to money
And the cold cities call us they need us to keep making distance
of all we could have been and all we are
We take our own children to the market
You work hard to be used and to be discarded
We prepare ourselves to be kind and to be deserted

Your love
is a falling star

# Borne

You fold back the light you look up look back down
In heavy black frames, the lenses of your glasses
glide with reflections of the pages you're reading
No one lives in your eyes
and the glance goes into nothingness
caribou appear in the snow among pines
and the mountains come closer and peer at you
like gigantic owls

The trail of your silence leads me to your side
I lie down and kiss your hips
but other people are moving beside us
eventually they take us and scatter north south east and west
They'll never return with us
We dream we are together
never noticing the stillness of lakes between
each one of our heartbeats

In an unmanned village railway station
a light comes on at dusk
the cone of its radiance catches the edges of geranium petals
and the crystal wings of aphids
No one will come here, no train is due
The rails bear their emptiness
Strangers bear our kiss
The lines vanish
That is where everything goes

Now the night has no destination
I love you into my dreams
In our sleep we are taken
and like jellyfish travel for thousands of miles
borne by the currents of oceans
We wake into salt and rooms
Our own lives escape us

their deserts and skies too great for us to handle
One moment of love is the end of our strength
but our weakness is beautiful and razes hope to the ground
And when a fire such as this burns
it is more lovely than the building inside it
One day, a stranger remembers us
and in a deserted station
a light comes on

# Mobile

I love it when you wear your hair up.

I love the fine hair on the back of your neck —
the way it fans and curves,
a black cirrus.

*I love the way you look at me
as if you have arrived somewhere
after a long journey.*

My life had grown peaceful and cold.
It was as if my heart were translucent
like ice on a river.

In a few minutes, I will see you again.
How I've missed you.

With the grace of young ferns,
the blind inevitability of frost.

As the words drift slowly
through the years and the miles,

and small kisses tremble and shift
nervous and fragile
like thistledowns caught in the rain.

So the heart prepares itself for love
like a teenager fallen asleep on a train
with her hand
still clutching her mobile.

# Tadpole

Sometimes the evening light in spring is so soft and subtle
it seems to tremble as if it might open
and let us in
Love haunts the coming night and she's calling you
Something immense and strange happens to be close
we may just be on the edge of kissing
It's so quiet if we speak now
our voices would resonate in the superclear air
Like a shadow falling over our shoulder
we can sense it
but not see nor hold
something so tender
It drifts nearer
but its nature is in passing
like an airliner gliding above butterflies
the flow of empty ripples across a pool
a frog swimming among tadpoles

## Cusp

You're the one who's been in the water.
The others on the beach didn't go in
so they seem okay with the temperature,

but you're cooler than them
and you shiver a little.
You can feel goosebumps beginning to form.
A delicious quiet falls,
and you think of tomorrow, when you will be young.

In this way, the stars begin to come out
with the softness of ice melting.

www.ingramcontent.com/pod-product-compliance
Lightning Source LLC
Chambersburg PA
CBHW021327190426
43193CB00039B/408